WHALE RESCUE

WHALE RESCUE

Changing the Future for Endangered Wildlife

ERICH HOYT

FIREFLY BOOKS

A FIREFLY BOOK

Published by Firefly Books Ltd. 2005

First printing

PUBLISHER CATALOGING-IN-PUBLICATION DATA (U.S.)

Hoyt, Erich.
Whale rescue : changing the future for endangered wildlife / Erich Hoyt. —1st ed.
[64] p. : col. photos. ; cm. (Firefly animal rescue)
Includes index.
Summary: An exploration of whales, their various habitats, the threat of extinction, and the conservationists who are working with them.
ISBN 1-55297-601-7
ISBN 1-55297-600-9 (pbk.)
1. Whales — Juvenile literature. 2. Endangered species — Juvenile literature. I. Title. II. Series.
599.5 22 QL737.C4H69 2005

LIBRARY AND ARCHIVES CANADA CATALOGUING IN PUBLICATION

Hoyt, Erich
Whale rescue : changing the future for endangered wildlife / Erich Hoyt.
(Firefly animal rescue)
Includes index.
ISBN 1-55297-601-7 (bound).—ISBN 1-55297-600-9 (pbk.)
1. Whales—Juvenile literature. 2. Endangered species—Juvenile literature.
3. Wildlife conservation—Juvenile literature. I. Title. II. Series.
QL737.C4H695 2005   j599.5   C2004-906071-6

Published in the United States by
Firefly Books (U.S.) Inc.
P.O. Box 1338, Ellicott Station
Buffalo, New York 14205

Published in Canada by
Firefly Books Ltd.
66 Leek Crescent
Richmond Hill, Ontario L4B 1H1

Design: Ingrid Paulson

Printed in Canada by Friesens, Altona, Manitoba

*The Publisher acknowledges the financial support of the Government of Canada through the
Book Publishing Industry Development Program for its publishing activities.*

TABLE OF CONTENTS

Giants of the sea. 6

Where do whales live? 8

The story so far 10

Gaining the upper hand. 12

A world divided. 14

Whale of a journey 16

ON THE FRONTLINES: Amazing grays. 18

A whale for the counting. 20

ON THE FRONTLINES: Humpback comeback 22

Humpback songs. 24

AT WORK: Robin Baird 26

AT WORK: Out of the blue 28

Thar she blows. 30

AT WORK: Hal Sato 32

Sleuths of the high seas 34

Going too far 36

ON THE FRONTLINES: Sperm whales 38

Cutting out the noise. 40

Poisoning the seas 42

AT WORK: Giuseppe Notarbartolo di Sciara 44

Whale reproduction 46

ON THE FRONTLINES: Saving right whales 48

What a tangled net. 50

AT WORK: Stormy Mayo 52

Thanks, but no tanks 54

The future for whales 56

Fast facts. 58

How you can help 60

Index 62

Photo credits 63

Author's note 64

GIANTS OF THE SEA

Whales are magnificent examples of life—beautiful, enormous, intelligent and highly social.

The largest of the cetaceans (pronounced se-TAY-shuns), a group of mammals that also includes dolphins and porpoises, whales are divided into two groups. Baleen whales—such as humpback, right, fin and blue whales—feed on anything from tiny plankton to small schooling fish, which they strain from the sea. Toothed whales—such as the sperm whale and orca—hunt mainly fish and squid. Orcas also take seals and other large sea creatures, including other whales.

Whales are champion swimmers and divers. They have a thick layer of blubber to protect them from the cold. The blue whale, at up to 110 feet (33.5 m) and 214 tons (190,000 kg), is the largest animal that has ever lived.

People have hunted whales for centuries, and several species—blue, humpback, right, gray and bowhead—were close to extinction before most of the killing finally stopped. Yet every year, Japan and Norway continue to harpoon more than a thousand whales, and the animals face other threats from overfishing, entanglement in fishing gear, boat traffic and pollution.

Life in the 21st century can be hazardous and uncertain for the giants of the sea, but conservationists are fighting hard to make a place for whales.

< A 45-ton humpback whale leaps high above the water. Over several centuries humpback whales, as well as other baleen whale species, were hunted nearly to extinction.

WHERE DO WHALES LIVE

Whales live in almost every ocean. Some species, such as gray whales, prefer shallow coastal waters. Others, notably sperm whales, are found above deep ocean canyons. Humpback whales and orcas live in both shallow and deep waters, depending on what they are feeding on, their behavior and the time of year.

Like many animals, whales travel in search of food, mates, familiar surroundings or safe areas in which to raise their young. The journey from the tropics, where many baleen whale species breed and calve, to polar waters where they do most of their eating, can be as long as 5,000 miles (8,000 km)—all accomplished on an empty stomach.

The longest migrations are undertaken by baleen whales such as humpbacks. In the eastern Pacific, for example, humpbacks migrate between Antarctica and the waters off Colombia and Panama, crossing the equator. Grays swim along almost the entire west coast of North America as they migrate from Mexico to Alaska. In the North Atlantic, certain northern right whales migrate from Florida or Georgia to the Bay of Fundy, while humpbacks travel from the Caribbean to the Gulf of Maine, the Gulf of St. Lawrence or Davis Strait, off Greenland.

Toothed whales (sperm whales and orcas) range over wider areas, but do not migrate as far as baleen whales.

<   Most belugas live in the Arctic Ocean. A few hundred live in the St. Lawrence River.

THE STORY SO FAR

about 6000 BC Native people of northern Canada and Alaska begin hunting whales for meat and oil.

about 3000 BC Earliest recorded whaling in Labrador and Newfoundland.

2200 BC Rock carvings in Norway depict whalers hunting in canoes with spears.

400–1000 AD Inuit whaling spreads from Alaska across Canada to Greenland.

11th century The world's first commercial whalers, the Basques of western Europe, create an industry from hunting right whales.

1607 British and Dutch whalers begin hunting the bowhead whale off Spitsbergen.

1640s New England colonists start hunting 'local' humpback whales.

1712 A Nantucket Island captain accidentally discovers a prime sperm whale area, creating a market for yet another species of whale.

1860s Steam ships and explosive harpoons emerge, allowing whalers to kill with far greater efficiency.

1874 A prominent whaling captain predicts doom for the gray whale, writing that before long "it may be questioned whether this mammal will not be numbered among the extinct species."

1904 Whalers explore Antarctic waters and discover hundreds of thousands of whales, which are soon slaughtered in huge numbers. By 1970, 369,000 blue and 720,000 fin whales will be killed in the southern hemisphere alone.

1946 The International Whaling Commission is formed, but it does little to control the killing until the 1970s.

1960s Whales become a symbol of the budding conservation movement, and the general public begins pressing for an end to commercial whaling.

1972 The US, Canada, Britain and Australia ban whaling.

1986 The world stops commercial whaling, but Japan and Norway protest and soon resume the hunt.

∧ Spermaceti, the waxy substance which whalers obtained from the sperm whale's head, is ground and pressed to make oil.

A life-size blue whale, inflated in Mexico City, celebrates the Mexican government's 2002 designation of a whale sanctuary covering Mexico's national waters.

1993 Scientists reveal that Soviet whalers illegally killed more than 100,000 endangered whales between 1947 and 1972.

1994 The gray whale in the eastern North Pacific becomes the first species to recover fully.

1998 Whale watching surpasses the value of whaling as 9 million people a year spend more than US$1 billion on tours in nearly 500 communities.

2001–2004 Japan tries to block the creation of new international sanctuaries for whales in the South Pacific and South Atlantic. Ten countries respond by declaring their national waters as whale sanctuaries, covering more than half the South Pacific.

2004 A worldwide study reveals that more than 500 areas have now been established or proposed to conserve the critical habitat of whales. Still, pressures on whales are growing—from fishing conflicts, boat collisions, pollution, global warming and increasing whaling activity.

GAINING THE UPPER HAND

Early whalers who hunted with open boats and handheld harpoons faced enormous dangers. They were also limited to killing only slower, easier-to-catch species. By the late 19th century, technology made whaling easier and safer—for humans, that is.

In 1868, a Norwegian popularized the explosive harpoon, which was tipped with a grenade and fired from a cannon. Around the same time, steam-driven ships replaced traditional sailing ships. With these advances, sperm, humpback and the remaining right and bowhead whales began to fall rapidly. And for the first time, whalers caught up with faster species such as the fin, sei and—the ultimate prize—the blue whale.

^ The humpback whale was one of the first species to suffer severe declines from whaling.

In 1904, whalers reached the final frontier—Antarctica. This untouched feeding ground for hundreds of thousands of whales proved to be the richest jackpot of all. For the first two decades, Antarctic whaling was conducted from islands in the Southern Ocean. By 1925, massive factory ships were hauling the whales on board to be processed. The pace of whaling picked up.

In 1931, the peak year, 29,400 blue whales were killed in the southern hemisphere. By the 1950s, few blues were left, and the whalers turned to fin whales, which were killed in large numbers through the 1960s. Sei whales were next on the list until they too were endangered.

For more than nine centuries, whaling occurred without thought of the future. In the 1900s alone, more than two million were killed, and by the end of the century, populations of blue and humpback whales had been devastated—their original numbers reduced to 10 percent or less.

This is the situation researchers and conservationists face today. The oceans are a much different place from when whales were masters of the seas.

< In the late 19th century, the explosive cannon-fired harpoon, along with faster boats, put most of the world's whales within easy reach.

A WORLD DIVIDED

In the 1930s, a few countries agreed to regulate whaling, and in 1946 the International Whaling Commission (IWC) was formed—not to conserve whales for their own sake, but rather to divide the spoils. For decades, the hunt moved from one species to another, till each in turn approached extinction. Protection—beginning with right and gray whales in the 1930s—only came when a species had declined so much that it was no longer profitable to hunt anyway.

By the late 1960s, the public became aware of the slaughter, and pressed their governments for change. Whales became a symbol of the budding environmental movement, and by 1972, American, Canadian, British and Australian whalers had handed over their harpoons to museums.

In 1982 most of the world's nations voted to stop commercial whaling by 1986. But some countries have continued: Japan has hunted minke whales, and more recently Bryde's, sei and sperm whales, supposedly for scientific research. Iceland began a similar practice in the late 1980s, then stopped and only resumed in 2003. Norway has ignored world opinion, killing hundreds of minke whales each year in the North Atlantic.

∧ In the Faeroe Islands, the sea runs red with the blood of pilot whales and dolphins. The centuries-old annual hunts use small boats to drive the whales into the shallows where they are killed for meat.

At the same time, the US, Canada and Russia have continued to allow aboriginal people to hunt whales. Some hunts are managed and whale populations have remained steady, while other native hunts have poor or no management.

In all, since 1986, more than 25,000 whales have been killed through legal loopholes.

In the 1930s, a harpooned whale is hoisted high on the dockside, ready for flensing.   >

WHALE OF A JOURNEY

Whale species are made up of populations—groups of individuals that are related, although sometimes only distantly related. Each population tends to live and mix together in the same areas, rarely interbreeding with others of the same species.

The more populations a species has, the more insurance it carries against extinction. Research over the past few decades has tried to determine what makes up a whale population.

One of the challenges of studying whale populations is charting their marathon voyages. Whales undertake some of the longest migrations of all sea animals—some pass through the waters of a dozen countries in a typical year. South Pacific humpbacks spend the summer feeding around the Antarctic before ranging north some 5,200 miles (8,350 km) to cross the equator into the waters off Colombia and Panama. This is the longest migration of any mammal.

How long does it take a whale to migrate? Of course, it depends on the species and the distance. Humpbacks in the North Pacific, which are probably faster than right whales, but not as fast as blue or fin whales, have taken as few as 36 days to swim from Hawaii to southeast Alaska. Researchers learn the secrets of migration through matching individuals from photographs or genetic samples taken throughout their range, or by tagging individual whales and following them by satellite.

∧ The distinctive black and white patterns, found on the underside of the humpback whale's tail, are like "fingerprints" and can be used to identify individual animals.

< A humpback whale mother and calf arrive on the warm breeding grounds of Hawaii.
The new calf may have been born during or after the migration from Alaska.

Few whales have come as close to extinction as grays. In the 1800s, their breeding grounds were discovered in the shallow lagoons of Baja California, Mexico, where they were easily cornered and killed—so quickly that gray whales were thought to be extinct in the early 1900s. However, some survived and began a long, slow recovery.

The habit that made gray whales vulnerable—their tendency to stay close to land—now began to work in their favor. By the mid-1940s, students at the Scripps Institution of Oceanography in California started counting migrating grays from the tops of buildings. In the late 1950s, the counts became part of whale watching tours from land and by boat. Gray whale awareness was growing, and the numbers were climbing. Soon California adopted the gray whale as its state marine animal.

By 1994, the story was out: the Eastern Pacific gray whale had become the first whale to return to its original numbers—an estimated 23,100 animals. It was removed from the US list of endangered wildlife. What had saved it was protecting habitat, controlling whaling and giving the species time to recover.

Besides the well-known gray whales that migrate along the Pacific coast of North America, another population—the western Pacific or Asian gray whale—moves between the waters of the Russian Far East and probably China. Since 1995, scientists have photographed and taken skin samples of these rare whales, only 100 of which are left.

The western Pacific grays were declared critically endangered and a marine sanctuary has been approved to protect them, but the oil companies are ignoring the boundaries recommended by scientists.

A gray whale stirs up the mud as it "bottom feeds" on tubeworms and various shrimp-like > crustaceans called amphipods.

A WHALE FOR THE COUNTING

When studying any large mammal, researchers must learn to identify individuals. In 1971, American researcher Roger Payne took his family to Patagonia, at the bottom of South America. They spent their days watching right whales on their late-winter mating grounds in the South Atlantic. Every time a right whale surfaced, they tried to take sharp pictures. Using these photos, they learned to identify the whales from the whitish patterns of roughened skin on the head.

Other researchers developed similar techniques—identifying gray whales from scars or other unique markings on the head and back, humpbacks by the black and white patterns on the underside of their tail flukes, and orcas mainly from marks on the rear edge of the dorsal fin. A sharp photograph, with the precise place and date it was taken, can be matched to future photographs during the whale's lifetime. This information can provide a basic count of individuals and help track their movements.

Researchers have also studied humpback songs and have attached electronic tags to whales so they use radio or satellites to monitor movements and activity patterns. Older tags were attached using bolts or other devices, but new rubber suction tags don't disturb the whales as much.

Another tool is biopsy sampling—collecting pieces of skin. After they leap, whales sometimes leave skin in the water. In other cases, scientists fire a small dart into a whale's back to collect a plug of skin and blubber. They can then analyze the DNA to identify the individual, learn the whale's sex and how it is related to others in the population, as well as measure any contaminants in the body.

∧ In Abrolhos National Marine Park, a protected archipelago off mainland Brazil, Marcia Engel uses a crossbow to obtain a tiny skin sample for biopsy research.

< One of the fathers of modern whale research, Roger Payne took his family to live with southern right whales found along the coast of Patagonia, Argentina, in the 1970s.

A breaching 45-ton (40,000 kg) humpback makes for one of the more joyful experiences in nature. Indeed, these whales' flamboyant habits and tendency to tag along with boats no doubt made them easy pickings for whalers.

∧ A humpback whale starts to flip its tail flukes high above the water before a deep dive.

Fortunately, though, these traits have also made them fairly easy to study. Humpbacks were one of the first whales to be studied using photo-ID in the 1970s—researchers photographed the underside of their tails, which have intricate patterns ranging from nearly all black to all white and everything in between.

In the early 1990s, scientists from seven countries began a census of humpbacks throughout the North Atlantic using tail photographs, as well as skin samples to obtain genetic profiles. They reported recently that humpbacks in the North Atlantic are back to around 11,000, probably a significant portion of the number that existed prior to whaling. In 2004, scientists from Russia, Japan, Mexico, Canada and the United States started working together on a similar study of humpbacks in the Pacific Ocean.

A humpback whale breaches, showing off its long, up to 5-m (16-foot) long flippers, the longest appendages in the animal kingdom. After centuries of decline, the number of humpbacks in some areas of the world has increased.

The whales tend to go back to the same areas year after year—mothers bringing their calves, calves growing up and mating, and then bringing their calves. In the North Atlantic, the humpbacks spend their summers in the waters of Massachusetts, Maine, Nova Scotia, Newfoundland, Labrador, Quebec, Greenland, Iceland and Norway. In winter, most head for the waters of the Dominican Republic. Before whaling, humpbacks also wintered in the Cape Verde Islands, off Africa, and in the eastern Caribbean. It will take decades, maybe centuries, before we know if humpbacks will return in any number to these former breeding areas. Some places they will probably never go back to. Off South Georgia, in the South Atlantic, for example, humpbacks were whaled heavily and have not been seen since.

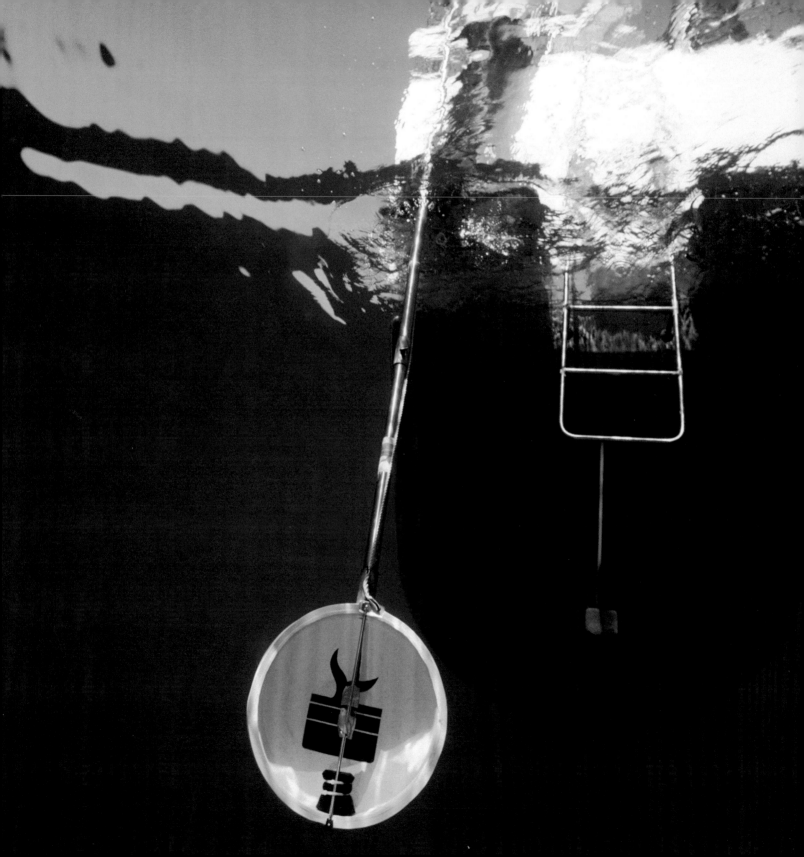

HUMPBACK SONGS

Male humpback whales have long been known to sing complex songs that last 5 to 30 minutes and include repeated phrases that create a theme. Several themes, incorporating sounds from low rumbles and roars to high-pitched squeals, are found in every song. But what do the songs mean? If the songs are important in courtship or when choosing mates, then there may be another reason for reducing noise pollution in the oceans.

"Our understanding of humpback song is in the early stages," says Jim Darling of the West Coast Whale Research Foundation. Darling has studied humpbacks and grays since he first discovered whales as a surfer off Vancouver Island in the early 1970s.

∧ Male humpback whale sings on the breeding grounds around Maui, Hawaii.

Researchers know that the songs change gradually during the breeding season and that all the humpbacks in each population are singing the same song. The male humpbacks usually assume a "singing posture," staying still with their head down, or traveling slowly. The songs are loud—in fact, the low parts can travel hundreds of miles through deep ocean basins.

Are the songs attracting females? Some researchers have observed females joining singers. Yet Darling says there is no evidence that females choose singers as mates. Instead, he says that how a male sings may show how he fits in or ranks among other males on the breeding ground.

Meanwhile, in seas once rendered nearly silent, the humpbacks just keep on singing. In more than 20 years, the whales have never gone back to previous songs. They are continually evolving new combinations of sounds, new melodies and rhythms.

< A directional underwater microphone, or hydrophone, is used to find whales and record their songs and other sounds.

Growing up in Victoria, British Columbia, Robin Baird used to watch—and listen to—groups of orcas as they puffed by the waterfront. Baird went on to do his PhD on the local killer whales but since then he has worked on some 29 species of whales and dolphins in ten different countries. "I'm constantly amazed at how little is known about most species, and I am excited by discovering new things," he says.

∧ In two seasons working off Hawaii, Robin Baird attached several dozen suction cup radio tags to humpback whales.

One of Baird's specialties has been using radio tags and "crittercams," which he attaches to the whales using suction cups. In this way he can learn more about how deep they dive, where they go and how far they travel. Recently, Baird went to Hawaii to find out how deep humpback whales dive on their breeding grounds. This is an important question, because the waters around Hawaii are becoming noisier and noisier. There is already a submarine torpedo testing range near Maui, and there are plans for experiments that would put loud, persistent sounds into the water. "High-intensity sounds contribute to strandings and may have affected a number of whale populations," says Baird. The question is, are humpbacks bothered by all the sounds? If the humpback is only a shallow-water species, the whales wouldn't be disturbed by the mainly deep-water sounds.

Baird used suction-cup radio tags—which he had already tried on orcas—to study humpback behavior without harming or greatly disturbing the animal. The suction cup tag is a gentle, inexpensive tool for learning about whales over the several hours or days before it falls off.

Humpback whale with a radio tag attached to its back. The whale carries the tag for hours or even days, sending back signals that reveal how deep the animals dive and where they go.

Working from a small boat with a crossbow, Baird managed to attach several dozen tags to the whales over two seasons. The results surprised him. He discovered that the female humpbacks dive up to 643 feet (196 m), nearly the maximum depth close to shore around Hawaii, and the males follow them down. Some males spend more than a quarter of their time below 330 feet (100 m).

Baird doesn't know why the humpbacks are doing so much deep diving, but one thing is certain: we had better cut the noise down.

Richard Sears spends most of his waking hours trying to get closer to the largest animal that's ever lived. From April to June, he visits Labrador and northern Newfoundland to watch blue whales feeding on krill as the icebergs drift past. By August, he moves to Quebec's Mingan Islands, in the northern Gulf of St. Lawrence, to meet groups of feeding blues. From August until at least October, he tracks the blues up the St. Lawrence River and by February he's on a plane to Mexico to study Pacific blue whales. Other years he spends a few days or weeks in Iceland or the Azores "in search of the big picture," as he says.

∧ Richard Sears works on a database of tens of thousands of blue whale photographs, trying to identify and match blue whales seen in different years, or even the same years in different parts of the North Atlantic.

Some scientists thought Sears was crazy when he and two friends began the blue whale study in 1979. None had university degrees in whale research, and scientists told him that blue whales were unsuitable for photo-ID. Sears and company proved them wrong. They learned to find and photograph blue whales in fast, small boats, identifying them from the splotchy pigment patterns on the backs and sides.

Taking tens of thousands of photographs, Sears and his team have been able to document 463 different blues in the North Atlantic. In recent years off Iceland, Sears has found as many blue whale calves in six weeks as he has seen in 25 seasons in the St. Lawrence. He wonders whether this is because contaminant levels for blues are much lower in Iceland, or whether the Iceland population is simply larger and more productive.

A blue whale can be individually identified from the splotchy patterns of its head and body. Here, a blue whale spouts before rolling through the water and diving deep.

Blue whales feed on tiny shrimplike creatures called krill. The good news is that krill stocks are healthy worldwide, and they're not being overfished. Also, blues are fast, elusive, wide-ranging—all of which can be survival traits. They seem to prefer deeper waters where krill generally carry lower contaminant loads. But our optimism may be rooted in ignorance. The mysteries about blue whales greatly exceed the known facts.

THAR SHE BLOWS

Getting close to the largest animals that have ever lived, meeting them as individuals, learning about their mysterious lives in the wild and helping to save them—that's the appeal of whale watching.

Many endangered animals are too difficult to find, or too precarious to allow wildlife tourism. But whale watching has succeeded beyond all expectations. More than 9 million people a year now spend US$1 billion on whale watching tours, providing income and conservation benefits for nearly 500 coastal communities around the world.

It has even caught on in the whaling countries of Japan and Norway. Many young people in Japan have never eaten whale meat and are more interested in seeing whales alive. Over the past decade, more than a million Japanese have watched whales in their own country.

"Whales offer some of the best arguments we have to save species and habitats," says biologist Miguel Iñíguez from Argentina. Whale watching attracts tourists who spend a lot of money, ideally with little impact on the environment. The goal is to make them conservationists after they've met the whales.

Whale watching can also help research. Richard Sears has funded most of his work by offering blue whale watching holidays where participants even assist with the research by taking photographs, helping to spot whales, or recording data.

If you'd like to take a tour, make sure it's run by an organization that's working to help whales. Try getting a recommendation from a conservation organization, and make sure that there is a qualified naturalist, or nature guide, on the boat.

< Off Cape Cod, in New England, whale watchers can see feeding humpback whales from April to October. Whale watching tours bring people to meet whales and dolphins off the east and west coasts of the US and Canada and many other countries around the world.

31

AT WORK | HAL SATO

As a girl growing up in Tokyo, Haruko "Hal" Sato wanted to be an orca trainer in an aquarium. She saved her money and at age 17 visited northern Vancouver Island, British Columbia. There she met both orcas and minke whales, and became determined to learn more about wild whales and to devote her life to working with them.

∧ Hal Sato studies orcas in Russia and minke whales in her native Japan. She also guides whale watch tours to show Japanese the pleasures of whale watching.

At that time, in the mid-1980s, whales in Japan were mainly considered food. "I wanted to show Japanese people another view of whales," says Sato. She began writing articles, taking photographs and translating English articles and books.

Sato is small, but she's very strong and passionate when it comes to whales. She has a gift for being able to talk to and work with a wide range of people. When whale watching started in Japan in 1989, Sato soon became a naturalist guide, working with fishermen who were offering tours in a small southern town.

In 1999, Sato began working on a long-term research project on the orcas of the Russian Far East. This time she was helping to encourage and inspire young Russian students to study and help save orcas. While this project continues, Sato has also now started her own whale watching business in Hokkaido, off northern Japan. Of course, with Sato it's much more than an ordinary tour—participants learn about the local ecology and share in the fun, adventure and even the research.

Minke whales can be individually identified by the splotches of pigment especially on their sides and back. Japanese hunt minke whales in the North Pacific and the Antarctic, and Norwegians hunt them in the North Atlantic.

Using photo-identification, Sato has come to know some of the minke whales around eastern Hokkaido. She knows that minkes are not the most endangered whale, but she also knows that whaling took one species after another until minkes were the only baleen whales with healthy population levels.

Is it depressing to get to know minke whales that your countrymen are killing not far from your study area? Sato tries to be optimistic. "I love these whales and I love to see the smiles on the faces of the people when they meet them. I know it takes time, but I feel that things are slowly changing." She hopes that one day soon the killings will stop. Meantime, the minke whales have a champion in Hal Sato.

SLEUTHS OF THE HIGH SEAS

International bans on whaling have helped protect the most vulnerable whale species. As long as there is money to be made, illegal whaling will continue. Conservationists argue that whaling on the high seas is impossible to police, and that whalers will take anything and everything until it is gone. That's why, these days, whale conservationists have to be detectives, too.

In 1993, Russian scientist Alexei Yablokov announced that the former Soviet Union had been killing whales illegally for years, often smuggling them into Japan. No one was too surprised, but when Yablokov bravely made the numbers public, the world was astonished. Between 1947 and 1972, more than 100,000 whales were secretly killed, including more than 45,000 humpbacks, more than 9,000 blue whales, and even 3,872 extremely endangered right whales. These tragic numbers help explain why these species were declining even when they were supposed to be protected.

∧ High-priced whale products are available in a Tokyo meat market.

In other detective work, conservationists began buying and sampling whale meat in Japan, where only four large whale species are allowed to be caught and sold. With techniques similar to the DNA fingerprinting used to catch criminals, scientists discovered that, besides the permitted whales, the markets were selling blue, fin, sei, humpback and other species, some of them endangered. Some of the meat is probably frozen flesh from whales killed before 1986. Some is likely from whales caught by accident (or sometimes on purpose) by large fishing boats.

More than anything, this detective work shows how hard it is to control the hunting, trading, and sale of whale products, and why the best way to protect the animals is to ban whaling completely.

< Russian whaling ships caught minke whales in the Antarctic before the whaling ban in 1986.

GOING TOO FAR?

Whale conservation groups use many methods to defend the oceans. The most drastic and controversial actions have been those of the Sea Shepherd Conservation Society.

∧ A demonstrator at the annual International Whaling Commission (IWC) meetings says "no" to the return of whaling.

Founded in 1977, Sea Shepherd is led by the burly, charismatic Paul Watson, who was once a member of Greenpeace. Today Sea Shepherd patrols the seas, sinking illegal whaling boats and driving through fishing nets, that can kill whales and dolphins. Watson and his team are determined to stop the activities of whalers, illegal fishers and polluters and, if necessary, disable their ships, but they don't want to hurt people. One of his most powerful weapons has been on-board cannons filled with cream-pie filling or stink bombs.

Few people shed tears when Sea Shepherd sinks pirate vessels that have been responsible for many whale deaths. But the group has also sunk whaling ships in Norway and Iceland, and this has made many people in those countries angry at all conservationists. Besides, the insurance money just buys new, better-equipped whaling ships.

Most conservation groups today, including Sea Shepherd, set more long-term goals for saving whales. They sponsor scientific projects, educate communities about conservation, and work to change government policies and laws. While getting the public's attention is important, much of the business of saving whales today goes on behind the scenes in international meetings and workshops that do not make headlines.

In an activity pioneered by Greenpeace in the 1970s, a whale protest is staged at sea, with > anti-whaling Sea Shepherd demonstrators trying to put themselves between the harpoon and the whale.

I t helps if sperm whale biologists are good sailors. In the early 1980s, shaggy, red-bearded Hal Whitehead and his young research team set out on a three-year sail across the Indian Ocean.

∧ Hal Whitehead listens for sperm whale "clicks", with headphones connected to a hydrophone.

The trip, sponsored by WWF-Netherlands, was the first attempt to meet the whales living in the newly created Indian Ocean Whale Sanctuary. The team met massive blue whales off Sri Lanka and the first Indian Ocean humpback whale singers recorded off Arabia, but their main quarry was the hard-to-find sperm whale, the animal with the largest nose and the largest brain on earth.

For the biologist, the nose was a mystery: What did the whale use it for? Was it for ramming prey or a way to help it float? And why such a big brain?

In the waters off Sri Lanka, they found a group of sperm whale mothers and babies, and over the next few years, they photographed and recorded their behavior.

When not hunting, the whales spend hours socializing, often at the surface, where they touch and caress each other. Mothers and young form tight, long-lived social units. By analyzing the DNA from skin collected after it fell off the whales, the team discovered that most of the whales that travel in these groups are mothers, grandmothers and sisters. Males leave the groups at about age six and move to cooler waters for hunting.

A female sperm whale surfaces for air before returning to feed in the deep water canyons around the Azores Islands.

Based at Dalhousie University in Halifax, Nova Scotia, Whitehead and his biologist wife Linda Weilgart have uncovered the big picture of sperm whale society, discovering that communication patterns are passed along the female line. The whales learn to use these sounds to keep in contact with each other and to find food in the deep darkness. All the sounds are made in their huge noses, focused through the spermaceti organ in their large heads.

As it turns out, those large noses are neither battering rams nor a method of keeping afloat—they're the instruments of sperm whale culture.

CUTTING OUT THE NOISE

On March 16, 2000, two minke whales and 14 beaked whales stranded on beaches in the northern Bahamas. Most were alive. Eight were returned to the sea and may have survived; the rest died. The autopsies showed the dead whales had ruptured eardrums.

That day, the US Navy was sending very loud, low sound pulses through the water. These sound pulses—routinely used by warships to detect submarines—were almost certainly the cause of the whale strandings.

Sound is a critical part of communication for humpbacks, orcas, blue and fin whales, and many other species. In the darkness of the deep sea, sperm whales produce patterns of clicks, called codas, for communication. They hunt by emitting clicks and listening to the reflected sound waves, which reveal the size and location of their prey. This technique is called echolocation, and it's similar to the sonar that submarines use to locate other underwater vessels.

∧ Bahamian children visit a stranded beaked whale.

Large male sperm whales also create a powerful crashing sound that researchers call the "big click," which sounds like an iron door clanging shut. It may be used to try to keep younger or inferior males away from potential mates—the larger the male, the slower and heavier the click.

Besides the navy sonar, very loud sounds are used to explore for oil. These two sound sources together present the most serious threats to whales. In recent years, oceanographers have also experimented with broadcasting loud, persistent sounds across the ocean to study temperature changes. This climate research may someday benefit whales through its findings, but not if it helps make them deaf in the process.

< In March 2000, 16 mainly beaked whales stranded on the beaches of the Bahamas. At least eight died. This "stranding event" occurred at the same time as the US Navy began testing a submarine detection system using loud sound pulses.

POISONING THE SEAS

In late 1987 and early 1988, 14 humpback whales mysteriously washed up dead along the shores of Cape Cod, Massachusetts. What had killed them?

It turned out to be tiny, poisonous plant plankton from what is called an "algal bloom." These toxic organisms can kill fish and mammals that ingest them—they can even be fatal to humans who eat shellfish—and the humpbacks had likely been eating mackerel carrying the toxin. Unfortunately, toxic algal blooms have become more common, and researchers believe they may be triggered by environmental changes, including pollution.

Some of the most harmful pollutants are PCBs, a group of chemicals that are known to cause cancer in animals. Orcas, which eat marine mammals and fish, carry heavier loads of these contaminants because the toxins get more concentrated as they move up the food chain to the top predators. An orca found dead in 2002 in the eastern North Pacific had among the highest levels of PCBs ever recorded in a whale or dolphin. The orcas off southern Vancouver Island and the belugas of the St. Lawrence also have high PCB levels. Their populations are not recovering, and researchers are looking at whether pollution is part of the cause.

It's difficult to show that contaminants are actually causing whale populations to shrink. Both orcas and belugas suffer from other problems. Orcas have been taken for aquariums in large numbers, while the belugas were hunted. Both have experienced habitat destruction, a reduction of prey and noise pollution from ship traffic. Any of these things, in addition to pollution, could be responsible for population decline.

A humpback whale dies on a Cape Cod, New England, beach in 1987, victim of a saxitoxin > suspected to have been carried by mackerel that they had been seen eating.

Giuseppe Notarbartolo di Sciara's career as a marine scientist had a rough start. At age three, he was mistakenly fed a rotten fish that almost killed him. Since then he has never been able to eat seafood, despite thousands of hours at sea.

Italian by birth, Notarbartolo studied sharks and rays in San Diego before returning to Italy, where he founded the Tethys Research Institute, which studies whales in the Mediterranean.

With so many threats to marine life in this busy sea, from drift nets to pollution and ship traffic, Notarbartolo became determined to create the first whale sanctuary in the Mediterranean. In 1999, after nearly a decade of hard work, the Pelagos Sanctuary for Mediterranean Marine Mammals was born. It was the first marine protected area to include international seas as well as the national waters of the three countries.

At the same time, Notarbartolo worked on a much larger project that will help conserve whales and dolphins throughout the Mediterranean and the Black Sea. He helped countries in the region agree to guidelines for pollution, fishing gear and whale watching, among other things. This agreement covers a huge area and brings together people with many languages, religions and cultures, and it's paving the way for future projects to protect marine life around the world.

∧ Giuseppe Notarbartolo di Sciara has worked to create marine protected areas and conservation agreements and to protect whales and dolphins in the Mediterranean Sea.

The Tethys Research Institute studies the resident fin whales of the Mediterranean which spend their summers in the waters off Italy, France and Monaco.

"When we started, there was almost no knowledge or interest in whales in the Mediterranean," says Notarbartolo. Today, the Mediterranean leads the world in whale conservation.

WHALE REPRODUCTION

The early biologists who accompanied whalers knew some basic facts about whale reproduction. They could look at the genitals to see if it was male or female. If female, they could examine the ovaries and learn how many pregnancies the whale had. They still couldn't determine the actual number of calves born, or the number that had survived to become adults.

It takes more time to learn from living whales, though the knowledge can go much deeper. Understanding reproduction is a key part of any conservation project.

To study reproductive behavior in the field, first you have to distinguish males from females. Animals traveling regularly with calves are clearly successful mothers. But females who are immature, past breeding or between calves, are difficult to distinguish from males. These days, to determine the sex of a whale, researchers sometimes dive beneath a whale to look at the genitals, while others collect skin that falls off naturally. In a laboratory, they can extract DNA from the skin and determine not only whether it is male or female, but other genetic information as well.

Researchers rarely see whales mating, but most have a few stories. Sexual behavior may be most commonly witnessed in the right whale. When a mature female starts to groan, males within several miles stop feeding, turn and race toward her. They don't fight, but will jostle to get close to her to mate. Male right whales have the animal world's largest testes at almost 2,200 pounds (980 kg) and the longest penises—11 feet (3.4 m) long. Females often mate with several males, one after the other.

Right whale females can calve as early as five years old, but the average is about 7 ½. Males must be at least 10 years old to get close enough to a female to mate— any younger and smaller and they're pushed away by larger males.

< Researchers have begun to learn the secrets of endangered right whales after spending decades with the southern right whale, off Argentina and Brazil, and the closely related North Atlantic right whale off the US and Canadian east coast.

Flying over the Bay of Fundy one August day in 1980, Scott Kraus saw 16 right whales, including two mother-calf pairs. To say these whales were rare is too optimistic. More than any other whale, the North Atlantic right whale was slaughtered until nearly all were taken.

∧ Researchers off northern Florida aided by the US Coast Guard, try to free an entangled North Atlantic right whale.

Tracking right whales around the Gulf of Maine, Kraus' team discovered spring feeding areas in Massachusetts Bay, late-summer feeding areas in the Bay of Fundy, and a courtship area in Roseway Basin, south of Nova Scotia. A few years later, the researchers found birthing grounds and mother-calf nurseries off Florida and Georgia.

Kraus began working with Canadian Moira Brown to obtain tissue samples of right whales. Poised on the bow of the boat, Brown fires small darts from a crossbow into the backs of the whales to obtain tiny plugs of skin and blubber, which are examined in the lab. Brown and others discovered five main breeding lines, or families, of North Atlantic right whales. Later, another researcher used this work to show that North Atlantic, North Pacific and southern right whales, all of which look alike, are in fact three different species.

Researchers identified about 325 right whales in the North Atlantic, with an average of 12 new calves being added every year. But then there were just nine in 1998 and 1999 combined, and only one new calf in 2000. Still, the whales had some surprises in store. In 2001, the researchers counted 31 calves, the most ever in one year. And from 2002 to 2003, calf numbers continued well above the previous average.

Researchers from the Center for Coastal Studies, in Provincetown, Massachusetts, USA, try to inject an entangled North Atlantic right whale with a sedative in hopes of being able to remove the fishing line from the whale's jaw.

Despite this good news, researchers know that, given the number of mature females, there should be many more calves being born each year. A big part of the problem is that right whales are being hit by ships and dying from fishing gear entanglements.

> The researchers hope to find solutions that will allow more right whales to make it to breeding age, and to keep them alive once they get there. So far, they have succeeded in changing some shipping lanes and creating special protected zones where right whales are known to gather.

"Some researchers feel that North Atlantic right whales are destined for extinction," says Brown. "But if we can reduce human-related mortality, then they have a good chance. As long as they can keep up their end of the bargain and produce calves, I think the species can persist and grow."

WHAT A TANGLED NET WE WEAVE

In 1992, a North Atlantic right whale mother named Delilah, beloved by researchers, was struck by a ship and killed in the Bay of Fundy. Every death in a whale population of only 325 hurts, but to lose young breeding females is demoralizing.

All whale species are sometimes hit by ships or entangled in fishing gear. The injuries in some cases are superficial, though whales may carry life-long scars from boat propellers or from nets that cut and chafe. Others may carry parts of fishing lines, nets or hooks that interfere with swimming or feeding.

Of course, a whale hit squarely by a large ship has little chance of survival. In 2004, a freighter steamed into Los Angeles harbor carrying a dead fin whale ensnared on the bow. The captain failed to realize what had happened until the ship was examined in port.

Conservationists are encouraging ships to slow down, and are trying to move shipping lanes away from whales, but the industry often argues that changes would be too expensive. Researchers are also working with sonar companies to design devices that could detect whales and help prevent collisions.

Experts have developed methods of releasing whales from nets and other gear, and have also trained fishermen and other local people how to respond to emergencies. Some whales have been saved. Yet many other whales suffer such severe entanglements that the only thing researchers can do is monitor their slow deaths.

Clearly the best solution is a combination of careful fishing practices, laws to keep gear out of areas where whales are most susceptible, plus education and enforcement.

^ Whales such as this Mediterranean fin whale are increasingly being struck and killed by ever faster commercial ships including freighters, ferries and container ships.

< A humpback whale, entangled in a fishing net, waits for the net to be cut. Most entangled whales, however, drown.

On a snowy New England evening, the dark silhouettes along the shoreline reveal man and whale. As a life and death struggle goes on in the shallows, the man pats the whale tenderly on its head. He is waiting for help, and hoping the seas will stay calm and the light will last.

∧ Having attached a buoy and transmitter to an entangled North Atlantic right whale, "Stormy" Mayo's team return to the Coast Guard ship to begin the monitoring, waiting for the opportunity to try to free the whale.

To local residents, Charles "Stormy" Mayo is the fellow who saves whales found entangled in nets around Cape Cod. For two decades, the scientist whose grandfather was a Yankee whaler has put on a black wetsuit and splashed into the cold North Atlantic. Since 1984, he has helped to free more than 60 large whales.

"We start with a lot of patience and preparation," says Mayo, "because the effort may take many hours, sometimes days or even longer." His main technique is borrowed from an old whaling practice called kegging. Using a harpoon, hunters would attach large floats, or kegs, to whales to slow them down and prevent them from diving, before actually trying to kill them. Instead of using a harpoon, Mayo attaches floats to the net or line entangling the whale. Then, when the whale tires and is unable to dive, Mayo starts from the head, cutting free the lines with special knives mounted on the end of long poles.

"No two rescues are alike. Sometimes we can only attach a transmitter to the line and wait for more light or calmer seas to attempt another rescue. Some whales are rescued only months or years later." But with the transmitter attached, Mayo and his colleagues can monitor the whale's location and general health.

The powerful flukes of a humpback whale, when entangled in fishing gear, are the most difficult and dangerous part of the whale to free from nets.

Mayo has taught the method to some 15 teams along the east coast of the US and Canada, and he also argues for changes in fishing gear and nets so that fewer whales are caught.

Early on, Mayo realized that to save whales long-term he has to ensure their food supply is healthy. So he spends most of his days not looking for whales to free, but studying copepods, the tiny crustaceans that right whales feed on. Mayo's group has found that copepod-rich areas change from year to year, month to month, even within a day. So how do right whales know where to go? Mayo scratches his head. "This is what we need to find out. We're hoping that right whales are a lot more clever than anyone ever thought."

THANKS, BUT NO TANKS

In 2003, Russian captors netted 32 orcas against the advice of scientists. Aquariums in Japan and elsewhere wanted to buy the animals for about US$1 million each. Two young animals became entangled and a young female drowned. Another young female was flown to a Black Sea aquarium. She too died after a few weeks.

Orcas, or killer whales, are performing stars at marine aquariums in the United States, Canada, France and Japan. Millions of people every year watch them perform tricks. But does this help the conservation of the species in the wild?

Wild orcas—which are technically dolphins—live in tight family groups. The top predators in the sea, they use speed, strength, agility, intelligence and cooperation to hunt fish, squid and marine mammals, including other dolphins and whales, even the blue whale. Family groups are broken up when orcas are taken into captivity, and the concrete pools of aquariums are little more than bathtubs that allow only artificial social behavior. Deprived of their ability to hunt, they circle the pool, waiting to be thrown dead fish to eat.

∧ The famous orca Keiko is lifted from the water in Oregon to be flown to Iceland. Released into the wild, Keiko later died in November 2003.

In recent years, several aquariums have bred orcas successfully. For some endangered species, captive breeding can help conservation in the wild. But the situation is different for orcas—breeding is only to replace animals that die in captivity. Despite the return to the North Atlantic of Keiko, star of the Free Willy movies, there is no intention to restock populations with orcas bred in captivity. Many are the offspring of parents from different areas, even different oceans, so they no longer have "home waters" or wild family groups to return to.

THE FUTURE FOR WHALES

Several whale populations have returned from the brink of extinction thanks to the hard work of researchers and funding from conservation groups, foundations and governments.

Many species of whale, however, still face an uncertain future. North Atlantic and North Pacific right whales, and blue whales, despite huge efforts, may not survive this century. Scientists can only hope that new techniques or technologies will come along to aid conservation.

Many whales still face an uncertain future.

At the same time, researchers such as Robin Baird point out that conservation efforts must not be restricted to the well-known species. There are at least 25 species of lesser-known whales that have rarely been studied and for which basic information is unknown.

Once it was possible to aid an animal simply by leaving it alone to recover. The 21st century no longer offers that option. As the earth's human population grows, the pressure on the oceans—from boat traffic, overfishing, industrial development and pollution—will only intensify.

Will whales be a healthy part of this world in a hundred years? It depends not only on the work of scientists and conservation groups, but on the efforts of everyone.

Will we adopt ways of living that are gentler toward the earth, the sea and its wildlife? Will we begin to take a more active interest in conservation? Will we insist on a world that includes both humans and wild animals?

The answers to these questions will determine the fate of whales.

FAST FACTS

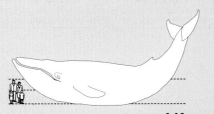

Scientific names
- 84 species form the order Cetacea, which includes whales, dolphins and porpoises
- toothed whales (including sperm whales and orcas) make up the suborder Odontoceti, while baleen whales (including gray, right, bowhead, humpback, blue, fin, sei, Bryde's and minke whales) belong to the suborder Mysticeti

Maximum size
- gray whales can reach 49 feet (15 m); humpbacks, 56 feet (17 m); right, bowhead, sei and sperm whales, about 60 feet (18.5 m); fin whales, 89 feet (27 m); blue whales, 110 feet (33.5 m) long and 200 tons (180,000 kg)
- female baleen whales are usually slightly larger than males; with most toothed whales, males are considerably larger

Life span
- gray whales are thought to live 40 years or more; humpbacks and sei whales at least 50; blue and right whales more than 70; fin whales and orcas more than 80; bowhead whales can live more than 100 years

Locomotion
- whales normally travel at speeds around 1 to 8 miles per hour (up to 13 kph), depending on the species
- the orca's maximum velocity is almost 18 miles per hour (28.5 kph); maximum sprinting speed for fin whales is almost 30 miles per hour (48 kph)

Reproduction	•	gestation is usually 11 to 12 months; possibly up to 18 months in sperm whales

Reproduction • gestation is usually 11 to 12 months; possibly up to 18 months in sperm whales

• only one calf is born at a time; females may calve as often as once a year (minke whales and sometimes humpbacks), while others (most humpbacks and right whales) calve no more than every two to four years. Orcas and sperm whales calve only every four to six years

• calves may suckle from 6 months to 2 years or more, depending on the species

Senses • at least four different whale species sing songs (notes repeated in a predictable way): bowhead, humpback, blue and fin whales

• humpback whales sing the longest and most complex songs in the animal kingdom; only the males sing, possibly as a prelude to mating

• the loud, low sounds of fin and blue whales can travel thousands of miles in deep water

• orcas communicate using calls that can be heard 10 miles (16 km) away

• orcas, sperm whales and other toothed whales use echolocation to navigate and hunt

• both toothed and baleen whales can see about as well as most land mammals, though not as sharply as primates; eye muscles allow considerable movement forward and backward and whales can move each eye separately

Diet • baleen whales generally feed on zooplankton (tiny animals), and small schooling fish strained from the water by the dense mat of hair growing on baleen plates in their mouths

• toothed whales can catch larger prey including fish and squid

• some orcas hunt, catch and eat minke and other baleen whale calves

HOW YOU CAN HELP

If you would like to learn more about whales or the projects designed to protect them, contact one of the following organizations or visit their Web sites:

Whale and Dolphin Conservation Society
www.wdcs.org
www.cetaceanhabitat.org

Brookfield House, 38 St Paul Street, Chippenham, Wiltshire United Kingdom SN15 1LY
Phone +44 (0)1249 449500
A leading funder of whale research; its Web site includes information on responsible whale watching tours, opportunities to "adopt" whales and dolphins, and protecting whale habitat around the world.

WhaleNet
whale.wheelock.edu

This site includes award-winning resources for students and teachers.

Center for Coastal Studies
www.coastalstudies.org

P.O. Box 1036, Provincetown, MA U.S.A. 02657
Conducts research on humpbacks, right whales and others, and has a rescue team for whales that become entangled in fishing gear.

Mingan Island Cetacean Study
www.rorqual.com

Research Station, 378 Bord de la Mer, Longue-Pointe-de-Mingan, QC Canada G0G 1V0
Phone (418) 949-2845
Founded by Richard Sears, this group does research on blue, humpback, fin and minke whales in the Gulf of St. Lawrence.

Tethys Research Institute *www.tethys.org*	c/o Venice Natural History Museum, Santa Croce 1730 30135 Venezia, Italy Phone +39 0412750206 Offers the chance to participate in whale research in the Mediterranean.
International Fund for **Animal Welfare** *www.ifaw.org*	411 Main Street, Yarmouth Port, MA U.S.A. 02675 One of the leading supporters of whale research and conservation education.
World Wildlife Fund U.S. *www.wwf.org* and *www.panda.org*	1250 24th Street NW, Washington, D.C. U.S.A. 20037 Phone (800) CALL-WWF Encourages on the ground work with whales and other animals in many countries.
World Wildlife Fund Canada *www.wwfcanada.org*	245 Eglinton Avenue East, Suite 410, Toronto, ON Canada M4P 3J1 Phone (800) 26-PANDA or (416) 489-8800

INDEX

A algal blooms, 42
aquariums, marine, 42, 55

B Baird, Robin, 26–27, 56
baleen whales, 7, 9, 58, 59
beluga, 7, 9, 42
biopsy sampling, 18, 21, 38, 47, 48
blubber, 7
blue whale, 7, 10, 13, 17, 28–29, 35,
    56, 58, 59
bowhead whale, 7, 10, 13, 58
brain, 38
breeding grounds, 9
Brown, Moira, 48, 49
Bryde's whale, 14

C calves, 23, 38, 59
captive breeding, 55
cetaceans, 7
codas (clicks), 38, 41
conservation efforts, 10, 11, 14, 36
    encouraging careful fishing
      practices, 51, 53
    preventing collisions with ships,
      49, 51
    protected areas, 11, 44, 49
    whale watching, 11, 18, 31, 32
    whaling bans, 10, 14, 35
conservation groups, 36, 60-61
copepods, 53

D Darling, Jim, 25
Delilah (right whale), 51

di Sciara, Giuseppe Notarbartolo,
    44–45
diet, 7, 29, 59

E echolocation, 41, 59
extinction, species facing, 7, 13, 14,
    18, 48, 56
eyes, 59

F feeding grounds, 9, 13
females, 38, 47, 58, 59
fin whale, 7, 10, 13, 17, 58, 59
future, 56

G genitals, 47
gray whale, 7, 9, 10, 11, 14, 18, 21, 58

harpoons, 13
H humpback whale, 7, 9, 10, 13, 21, 35,
    58, 59
    and deep-water noise, 26–27
    comeback of, 22–23
    migration of, 17, 23
    song of, 21, 25, 59

I Indian Ocean Whale Sanctuary, 38
Iñiguez, Miguel, 31
International Whaling Commission
    (IWC), 10, 14

J Japan, 7, 10, 11, 14, 31, 32, 35

K kegging, 52

Keiko (orca), 55
killer whale. See orca
Kraus, Scott, 48
krill, 29

L life span, 58
locomotion, 58

M males, 38, 47, 58
Mayo, Charles "Stormy," 52–53
Mediterranean, whale conservation
    in, 44–45
migration, 9, 17
minke whales, 14, 33, 59

N noise pollution, 25, 26, 27, 41, 42
Norway, 7, 10, 14, 31
nose, 38, 39

O orca, 7, 9, 21, 32, 42, 55, 58, 59

P Payne, Roger, 21
PCBS, 42
Pelagos Sanctuary for Mediterranean
    Marine Mammals, 44
photo-identification, 17, 21, 22, 28, 33
pollution of oceans, 42
    populations, 17
ranges, 9

reproduction, 47, 59
R right whale, 7, 9, 10, 13, 14, 21, 35, 58, 59
    diet, 53